How Does God's Law Apply to Me?

Crucial Questions booklets provide a quick introduction to definitive Christian truths. This expanding collection includes titles such as:

Who Is Jesus?

Can I Trust the Bible?

Does Prayer Change Things?

Can I Know God's Will?

How Should I Live in This World?

What Does It Mean to Be Born Again?

Can I Be Sure I'm Saved?

What Is Faith?

What Can I Do with My Guilt?

What Is the Trinity?

TO BROWSE THE REST OF THE SERIES,
PLEASE VISIT: **REFORMATIONTRUST.COM/CQ**

How Does God's Law Apply to Me?

R.C. SPROUL

IR *Reformation Trust*   A DIVISION OF LIGONIER MINISTRIES, ORLANDO, FL

How Does God's Law Apply to Me?
© 2019 by R.C. Sproul

Published by Reformation Trust Publishing
A division of Ligonier Ministries
421 Ligonier Court, Sanford, FL 32771
Ligonier.org   ReformationTrust.com

Printed in China
RR Donnelley
0001018
First edition

ISBN 978-1-64289-123-2 (Paperback)
ISBN 978-1-64289-124-9 (ePub)
ISBN 978-1-64289-125-6 (Kindle)

Cover design: Ligonier Creative
Interior typeset: Katherine Lloyd, The DESK

Scripture quotations are from the ESV® Bible (The Holy Bible, English Standard Version®), copyright © 2001 by Crossway, a publishing ministry of Good News Publishers. Used by permission. All rights reserved.

Library of Congress Cataloging-in-Publication Data

Names: Sproul, R.C. (Robert Charles), 1939-2017 author.
Title: How does God's law apply to me? / by R.C. Sproul.
Description: Orlando : Reformation Trust, 2019. | Series: Crucial Questions No. 30
Identifiers: LCCN 2018036542| ISBN 9781642891232 (Paperback) | ISBN 9781642891249 (ePub) | ISBN 9781642891256 (Kindle)
Subjects: LCSH: Law and gospel.
Classification: LCC BT79 .S67 2019 | DDC 241/.2--dc 3
LC record available at https://lccn.loc.gov/2018036542

Contents

Chapter One

Oh, How I Love Your Law!

Where should a study of God's law and its role in the Christian life begin? Some might consider the Ten Commandments the place to start, while others would turn to the book of Deuteronomy. Perhaps very few people might think of starting in the Psalms, but that is precisely where our journey begins.

Psalm 119, the longest psalm in the Psalter, is a magnificent celebration of the law of God. It is an acrostic, meaning that it is divided into twenty-two stanzas, one for each letter of the Hebrew alphabet, with each line of a given stanza beginning with the same letter. The idea is that of an exhaustive celebration of the law—from A to Z, we might say. This notion of celebrating God's law may seem completely archaic in our day because we are familiar with the teachings of the New Testament. We rejoice in being redeemed from the law. As Scripture says, "The law was given through Moses; grace and truth came through Jesus Christ" (John 1:17).

As a result, we tend to consider the Old Testament law completely irrelevant to our Christian lives today. Against this modern-day backdrop of rampant disregard for the Old Testament law, we do well to consider the words of the psalmist:

> Oh how I love your law!
>> It is my meditation all the day.
> Your commandment makes me wiser than my
>> enemies,
>> for it is ever with me.
> I have more understanding than all my teachers,
>> for your testimonies are my meditation.
> I understand more than the aged,
>> for I keep your precepts.

I hold back my feet from every evil way,
    in order to keep your word.
I do not turn aside from your rules,
    for you have taught me.
How sweet are your words to my taste,
    sweeter than honey to my mouth!
Through your precepts I get understanding;
    therefore I hate every false way.
(Ps. 119:97–104)

This section of Psalm 119 does not begin by imparting information but by voicing an exclamation. The word "Oh!" expresses a sigh of profoundly deep feeling, and in this case, the feeling is one of affection.

Do we often hear Christians say, "The thing I love the most about my Christian experience is the law of God"? Do we hear people in the church today celebrate the depth of their affection for the law of God? The obvious answer is no. But as we explore the law of God in these pages, we should begin to ask why Christians don't have a greater appreciation for God's law.

What is it about Christ and His work that would cause us now to despise or ignore what was the focal point of delight in the lives of Old Testament saints? Perhaps it's the assumption that the Old Testament law is no longer relevant to New Testament Christians and has no bearing upon our Christian growth. We reason that the law was for Old Testament believers, not for us today. To us, the Christian life is Christ, not Moses; it's gospel, not law.

We are much more likely to hear Christians voice depths of passion with exclamations such as "Oh, how I love You, Jesus!" or "Oh, how I love You, Lord!" But how might the Lord Jesus respond to these sentiments? His words to the nascent church are likely the same words He would speak to us today: "If you love me, you will keep my commandments" (John 14:15).

For a Christian to say, "I once loved the law, but now I love Christ and ignore the law," is simply not to love Christ, because Christ loved the law. His meat and His drink, the Scriptures tell us, was to do the will of the Father (John 4:34). Jesus viewed His entire life as a mission to fulfill every single point of the law and to achieve perfect obedience to the commandments of God. His motive was not to keep a list of rules but to do the will of the Father. And the Father clearly expresses His will through His law.

Throughout Psalm 119, there is a constant interchange

between the words "law" and "word." Christians today may speak in glowing terms of their affection for the Word of God, but we have a tendency to divorce the Word of God from the law of God. However, that dichotomy is not evident in this psalm, where throughout we see the psalmist reciting his affection repeatedly both for the law and for the Word of God. Why did the psalmist love the law of God so much?

The first thing to note is that the law expressed God's commandments, that which He wanted His people to do. When kings, presidents, leaders, or others who sit in seats of authority utter a directive, their word is not to be challenged. They are the final court of appeals, so there is no room for discussion. Their word is law.

Has anything changed about God that we would disregard His directives? Is His word still law? Is He still as sovereign as He was in the Old Testament? Is the God of Israel and of the New Testament church a commandment-giving God? His word is law, and His law is His word, because His law expresses His will. And that will, that law, is sweeter than honey (Ps. 119:103).

The book of Psalms begins with this benediction from on high: "Blessed is the man who walks not in the counsel of the wicked, nor stands in the way of sinners, nor sits in the seat of scoffers" (Ps. 1:1). This verse refers to a person who does not live according to the patterns, customs, and general wisdom of ungodly people. Translated into modern-day language, it might read like this: "Blessed is the man who is not a conformist to the cultural customs and patterns of our own society, who doesn't follow the popular wisdom of our day." Here in Psalm 1, a blessing is pronounced upon people who don't do certain things. And what is the positive side? "But his delight is in the law of the LORD, and on his law he meditates day and night" (v. 2).

We might be tempted to rewrite this today and say, "Foolish is the man who delights in the law of the Lord and wastes his time meditating on it day and night." We might think that only a legalist takes delight in the law and spends more than five minutes a year meditating upon it. But God says, "Blessed is the man. . . ."

The psalmist goes on to say, "He is like a tree planted by streams of water that yields its fruit in its season" (v. 3). Imagine the Judean wilderness that the psalmist and his original readers would have been familiar with. Think of the dry shoot that comes out of the ground in that barren wasteland, where any foliage that lives must fight to survive against the beating sun and the parched earth every hour of every day. And in the distance, picture an oasis where the trees are lush, full, and heavy with fruit because they are planted by the stream. Or picture the mouth of the Jordan River and the trees that grow right next to it, whose roots go deep into the ground, absorbing the moisture and the nutrients. These trees are robust and plentiful in the fruit that they produce. So in effect, God says, "Blessed is the man who meditates on My law day and night. He won't be like a tree that's planted in the middle of the desert with one tiny little root struggling to survive. He will be like the tree planted by the rivers of living water, bringing forth fruit in its season."

If there is a secret that lies hidden from the view of the modern Christian, that secret is found in the books of the Old Testament—not just in the Law, but also in the Prophets and the Wisdom Literature—all of which together reveal the character of God. If we wonder why God seems foreign to us, like an alien or an intruder into our lives; if we stumble and grope in darkness trying to understand how to live in a relativistic age; and if we feel like pieces of chaff that the wind drives away with the slightest breeze; then we need to go back and consider the law of God.

In the pages to come, we will explore the nature of the law in the Bible, and particularly, in the Ten Commandments, also known as the Decalogue. How did it function in the life of Israel in the Old Testament? And what is the relevance of the old covenant law now that we are in the new covenant? Is there any application of the Old Testament law to our day?

Chapter Two

Against
the Law?

Some have suggested that we are living in perhaps the most antinomian era in the history of the church. This word *antinomian* comes from the Greek *anti*, which means "against," and *nomos*, which means "law." Antinomianism is the belief that the law of God—or at least the Old Testament law—is in no way binding or relevant to the Christian life today.

We frequently read in New Testament passages, such as those written by the Apostle Paul, that we are no longer under law but under grace. That is routinely taken to mean that we are no longer responsible in any way to conform to the law of the Old Testament because, it is argued, the Old Testament law was relevant only to people in the theocratic system of Israel, wherein the state was governed by God through the priesthood. All of that was supposedly done away with when Christ signaled the start of the new covenant and the establishment of the Christian church. After all, John says in his gospel, "For the law was given through Moses; grace and truth came through Jesus Christ" (John 1:17).

There are many people who believe that the New Testament has its own set of commandments, and that as Christians, we are obligated to obey the rule of Jesus Christ and the law that He gives to His people. But where does that leave the Old Testament law in terms of our Christian lives today?

Scripture itself reveals that certain elements of the Old Testament law have been abrogated. Take, for example, the ceremonial law of the Old Testament, which consists of the rites and rituals performed by Israel in the worship of God. The offering of sacrifices was not simply a suggestion that God gave to Israel. By His command, the Israelites were obligated to celebrate the Day of Atonement, prepare burnt offerings, and remain faithful to the ceremonies. These rituals, the New Testament tells us, were shadows or types of the final sacrifice that was to be offered once for all in the death of Jesus.

In fact, we see the struggle in the New Testament against those who were trying to influence the church to continue these ceremonies. These Judaizers insisted that the Old Testament rituals be continued in perpetuity in the New Testament church. That view was hotly contested, and it was fiercely resisted by the Apostle Paul in his letter to the Galatians as well as by the author of Hebrews. The rationale was this: once Christ offered the perfect sacrifice once and for all, reverting back to the types and the shadows would be to deny the fullness of light and the total fulfillment that had come in that perfect sacrifice. Therefore, the Christian church has made it clear that we are not to continue these cultic, ceremonial practices of the Old Testament.

We also see a segment of Old Testament law that consists of dietary laws. In these laws, God prescribed which foods the Israelites were allowed to eat and which foods were considered unclean. They were not allowed to eat pork, for example. But in the New Testament, when the church expanded to include gentiles who followed a different diet, the question of dietary laws became important. The Council of Jerusalem, recorded in Acts 15, addressed this issue. God had given Peter a vision in which Christ told him not to declare unclean things that He had made clean. As a result, the list of prohibited foods was greatly reduced by the Council of Jerusalem. The dietary restrictions established in the Old Testament were lifted in the economy of the New Testament. Therefore, Scripture clearly reveals two ways in which the laws of the Old Testament are no longer absolutely binding upon the lives of Christians today.

Historically, the church has sought to answer the question of whether Old Testaments laws are still binding today by drawing a distinction between the different types of Old Testament law. According to this view, the law is divided into three categories: the dietary laws, the ceremonial laws, and the moral laws. As helpful as those distinctions may be, we must keep in mind that for the Jew in the Old Testament period, all of the law was moral. It was a moral issue to Daniel, Shadrach, Meshach, and Abednego whether they obeyed the dietary laws of God while they were in exile. It was a moral issue for Israel whether it obeyed the ceremonial law. Yet the purpose in our day of distinguishing between the three is to communicate that there is still a substantive stratum of law in the Old Testament that seems to continue into the life of the New Testament church.

One of the most important texts on this topic appears in the Sermon on the Mount, where Jesus says, "Do not think that I have come to abolish the Law or the Prophets; I have not come to abolish them but to fulfill them" (Matt. 5:17). Similarly, the Apostle Paul, when he speaks in glorious terms of how we have been redeemed from the curse of the law and are no longer under the law, is careful to warn us against jumping to the very conclusion that antinomians do—that the law has been completely removed from any consideration in the life of the Christian.

In Romans 7, Paul says, "So the law is holy, and the commandment is holy and righteous and good" (v. 12). This attitude characterizes the whole tenor of the New Testament's teaching on the law. In the book of James, for example, James speaks about the royal law of obedience in the teachings of Jesus Himself. In this epistle, where many of the Old Testament laws are reiterated for the benefit of the Christian church, we see that the substantive content of the moral law of the Old Testament still plays a vitally important role in the New Testament community. But again, the question is, What exactly is that role?

As we consider these questions about the law, we must remember that the fundamental problem in all of creation is the problem of evil. The fundamental problem in our lives is the problem of sin, and sin and evil are both defined in light of the law. The fall of Adam and Eve was a transgression against the law of God. Absolute wickedness in the Scriptures is associated with lawlessness (1 John 3:4). And the supreme manifestation of evil incarnate is the man of lawlessness (2 Thess. 2:8–10). So when we deal with questions about the law of God, we are not dealing with peripheral matters or tangential questions, but something that goes to the very core of our lives as human beings who are called to live *coram Deo*—before the face of God.

Chapter Three

The Law as a Mirror

There was a fierce debate in the Middle Ages over God's relationship to the law. Is God outside of the law, or is there some law above God to which He owes obedience and allegiance? This controversy was known as the *ex lex* controversy—*ex* meaning "outside of" or "apart from" and *lex* meaning "law." Theologians strongly rejected the idea that God functions *sublego*—under law. If God is under some law outside of Himself, then that law would be higher than God, and God would no longer be God—the law would. Therefore, there is no law outside of God that imposes obligations upon Him.

But if that's the case, is God lawless? Can He do whatever He wants? If He is not *sublego*, then must He be *ex lex*—outside of all law and able to act in an arbitrary or capricious manner without any sense of order? The theologians of the Middle Ages rejected this idea as well. They offered instead a third alternative, namely, that God is a law unto Himself. This differs from the idea that God is *ex lex* in that the behavior of God is never lawless. The actions of God are always in conformity to the law of God's own nature and character, which is inherently righteous and eternally holy. All of His actions come forth according to who He is.

This is significant because when we are called to obey the law of God, that means that we are called to obey *Him*. We are not simply trying to conform to an abstract set of principles or a disembodied list of rules; we are trying to live in relationship to our God. We are trying to please Him. We are trying to do what He wants us to do. Part of the nature of God is that He has within Himself supreme and absolute authority, by which He can issue commands to His creatures. But this authority is not exercised arbitrarily.

It reflects His eternal, holy character. God can command only what reflects His nature, and since He is wholly good, He can command only what is good. And good is defined by His nature; He is not bound to a standard of goodness outside Himself.

The law we are called to obey is a law that comes from Him. It is *His* law. It is a law that defines a relationship—the relationship between the Creator and the creature, between the sovereign and the vassal, between the King and His subjects. Not only is it His law in the sense that it comes from Him, but most significantly, it is a law that comes from and reflects His own character. It reveals and displays His righteousness, and therefore, it makes known what righteousness is. Notice that order. It is not that we first have a sense of righteousness and then we see that God conforms to it. Rather, first there is God in His perfect character, who is the standard of righteousness, and all righteousness is the revelation of who He is.

Anytime we deal with an ethical issue in society, people debate the pros and cons on both sides. It seems there is no form of human behavior that someone hasn't risen up to defend. We have various arguments and rationalizations to defend all kinds of disobedience, ungodliness, and evil, and we argue constantly about what is right and what is wrong. Christianity and Judaism assert that there is an absolute standard. What is right and what is wrong is not a matter of relativity. Instead, the ultimate standard is the character of God, and this character is manifested in His law.

The Westminster Shorter Catechism defines sin as "any want of conformity unto, or transgression of, the law of God" (Q&A 14). Here the word "want" refers to lack. Sometimes this dual definition of sin is simplified by reducing it to two kinds of sins: sins of commission and sins of omission. A sin of commission occurs when we commit an action that transgresses the law of God. If God says, "You shall not," and we do it, we have violated the commandment and transgressed His law. A sin of omission is when God says, "You shall," and we fail to do what is required.

With both kinds of sin, we are dealing with a lack of conformity to a standard. We fail to live up to the standard. The New Testament says, "All have sinned and fall short of the glory of God" (Rom. 3:23). We fall short or fail to hit the mark we are required to reach. We miss that requirement when we transgress God's law or fail to keep it perfectly.

What if there were no laws at all? The catechism defines

sin in terms of a relationship to law. But what if there were no laws? Would that mean that we would not be guilty of sin if there were no law to transgress? The Apostle Paul says, "If it had not been for the law, I would not have known sin" (Rom. 7:7). However, elsewhere in Romans, Paul asks whether law existed before Moses. His answer? Yes, there was a law in effect. He says, "Death reigned from Adam to Moses" (5:14), and there wouldn't have been death had there not been sin. He argues that in addition to being engraved on tablets of stone at Sinai, God's law is revealed in nature and inscribed on the hearts of all (even pagans), so that everyone has some knowledge of the law of God, some awareness of what is right and what is wrong. Paul means in Romans 7:7 that knowing and breaking the written law of God renders one more culpable for sin because it means breaking additional, special revelation that the Lord gave to clarify His standards. He does not mean that people who do not have the Scriptures have no law at all or that knowledge of God's standards did not exist until He gave the law to Moses.

Therefore, when people argue over whether adultery, theft, and murder are wrong, they know in their hearts that such things are wrong. They are simply trying to quell their own consciences in order to live according to their passions. According to Romans, "Though they know God's righteous decree that those who practice such things deserve to die, they not only do them but give approval to those who practice them" (1:32). That only underscores the sinfulness of sin.

The idea of the sinfulness of sin was addressed during the Reformation when the Reformers address the usefulness of the Old Testament law for New Testament Christians. One of the most helpful contributions in this regard was made by John Calvin. In his *Institutes of the Christian Religion*, Calvin provided an exposition of what he called "the threefold use of the law." In other words, Calvin said that the Old Testament law is useful to the New Testament Christian in three distinct ways. First, the law functions as a mirror; second, it functions as a restraint; and third, which Calvin saw as the most important, the law functions as a revealer.

The first use of the law is as a mirror. A mirror allows us to see ourselves as others see us. It shows us what we look like. Sometimes it allows us to see that we look good, but sometimes looking in a mirror is dreadful—when it reveals to us our blemishes.

Calvin observed that we can use a mirror to tell us whether there's dirt on our faces, but how can we tell if there's a stain upon our souls? There is no mirror bright enough to penetrate to the core of our character. If we want to see an accurate reflection of our moral character, we need a mirror far more powerful than the ones we usually look into, and that mirror is the law of God. Otherwise, we can all too easily deceive ourselves into thinking that we are righteous people. We compare ourselves to others, look at human laws, and give ourselves a high score. But once we look into the perfect mirror, once we examine the law of God, we are devastated, because we see the darkness of our sin against the standard of perfect righteousness. We see the sinfulness of our sin.

We don't always enjoy looking in mirrors. We often don't like what we see as it relates to our physical appearance. Perhaps that's one reason we avoid the law of God: we don't want to look in that mirror. But we must look in that mirror, because what we see in it alerts us to our desperate need and drives us to the gospel. The mirror of the law of God is bad news, but until we look at ourselves in it, we will never understand the goodness of the good news.

Chapter Four

The Law as
a Restrainer

Most of us have heard the idea that you can't legislate
morality. But this is actually a nonsensical statement. If we mean to say that the government shouldn't
be involved in passing legislation that curbs, restrains,
or restricts human behavior or morality, there would be
nothing left for Congress to do except assign names to government buildings.

Think about it. Are we suggesting that there shouldn't
be laws against murder? Or is theft not a moral issue? What

does government do if not legislate morality (or, at least, its concept of morality)? In fact, the basic purpose of legislation is to enact laws that are heavily weighted with moral concern. For example, it is a moral issue how we drive our cars on the road because how we drive can hurt or harm others. The law puts restraints on our desires; otherwise, we might pose a danger to the safety and livelihood of those around us. The law takes away some of our freedom and establishes a speed limit to protect us and others from serious injury or death. Flouting these laws makes us culpable to a fine or imprisonment. In this and countless other ways, it is clearly the business of government to legislate morality.

Perhaps this idea originally came into vogue because we know that passing a law to prohibit a certain form of behavior is no guarantee that the behavior will be eliminated. For example, it is illegal in the United States to use or sell certain drugs, but we know that those laws have not stopped the rampant sale and use of illegal drugs. Yet the presence of laws that legislate morality does restrain evil in some measure. Without laws restricting certain behaviors, evil would abound more.

Most of us can think of movies or shows depicting life

on the American frontier before the establishment of law and order. This anarchic and chaotic frontier society was colloquially called "the Wild West." It was a dangerous place to live before the arrival of law enforcement. So, even in our own country's history, we see that the law comes in for the purpose of restraining evil.

The New Testament speaks of earthly governments as fulfilling this very function. God gives the power of the sword to human governments to restrain evil, for if evil is unbridled and unrestrained, society is impossible, and civilization becomes barbarian.

God's law serves as a restraint, but of course, it doesn't do so absolutely. Humans can disregard the law of God in the same way that we disregard earthly governments. Calvin said this about the law as a restrainer:

The second function of the law is this: at least by fear of punishment to restrain certain men who are untouched by any care for what is just and right unless compelled by hearing the dire threats in the law. But they are restrained, not because their inner mind is stirred or affected, but because, being bridled, so to speak, they keep their hands from outward activity, and hold inside the depravity that otherwise they would wantonly have indulged. Consequently, they are neither better nor more righteous before God. (*Institutes of the Christian Religion* 2.7.10)

This is an important point. If the only reason we obey the law is out of fear of punishment or dread of the consequences, and not because our hearts are inclined to please God, we are no better in the sight of God than the person who, with reckless abandon, violates His standards and His law.

The benefit of this restraint is part of what we call in theology God's common grace. Winston Churchill said that with all of its weaknesses, democracy is still the best form of government. He even went so far as to say that tyranny is better than anarchy. The worst form of government is no government at all, where there is no restraint and the common grace of God is obscured.

Common grace does not include the special or salvific grace of God by which people are brought into a saving relationship with Christ. Rather, common grace refers to the common welfare that God provides for His people. It is the sunshine and the rain that falls on the just and the unjust—the general, universal benefits that we receive from the hand of God. One of the benefits of common grace is the benefit of His law, which makes it possible for sinful people to live together without completely destroying one another. This is one benefit of the restraint of the law.

Ironically, as the Apostle Paul observes in the New Testament, even though the law restrains us from sin, because of the wickedness of our hearts, it sometimes also has the opposite effect. Sometimes, knowledge of the law actually inflames us to sin. We've heard the expression "Rules are made to be broken." We've seen children who have no desire to engage in certain behaviors until those behaviors are declared off limits. And suddenly, that's exactly what they want to do. There's something inherent in our depraved natures such that we take delight in breaking laws just for our own pleasure and amusement.

With respect to the first two uses of the law—as a mirror and as a restrainer—Calvin said that both fulfill the metaphor used in Scripture about the law as a schoolmaster that leads us to Christ (Gal. 3:24). When we look at the language the New Testament uses in this regard, we can easily be misled because the educational system today functions in a way that is much different from the way that it did in the ancient world. We are familiar with the concept of only one teacher in the classroom, but in the ancient educational system, there were two adult officials in the classroom. There was the teacher and there was the pedagogue, or the schoolmaster. The function of the schoolmaster was not to impart information but to be the disciplinarian. He was responsible to discipline the wayward students and cause them to give their attention to the teacher. This lies at the heart of the biblical analogy.

God speaks to us of the free remission of sins in the gospel, but like wayward students, we don't pay attention. If we had the tiniest understanding of the character of God and an understanding of our own character, we would realize how desperately we need a Savior. But we don't think we need a Redeemer. We think we're doing just fine. We think that God grades on a curve, that our works are adequate, and that our righteousness is lofty enough to satisfy the demands of a holy God. It is as though we're falling asleep while the gospel is being preached until the schoolmaster awakens us to our peril and demands that we give our attention to the teacher. The schoolmaster doesn't just nod in our direction. The schoolmaster, in this case the law, drives us to Christ. The more we look in the mirror, the more we look at the restraining aspect of the law, the more desperately we understand our need for the gospel.

The cavalier attitude we have toward the gospel today, as well as our willingness to compromise it, negotiate it, or ignore it, is inseparably bound up with our ignorance of the law of God. There is no schoolmaster in our classroom anymore.

Chapter Five

The Law
as a Revealer

Of Calvin's three uses of the law, the third is perhaps the most important: the revelatory use of the law. Of course, the first use of the law as a mirror involves the revelatory use of the law as well, in that it reveals to us the righteous character of God. This third use, however, relates to another dimension of revelation that comes to us by the law of God.

The psalmist called God's law a lamp to his feet and a light to his path, in that it sheds light on how to live a life that is pleasing to Him (Ps. 119:105). Christians often grapple with the question of what God wants us to do, how He wants us to serve Him. We are constantly bombarded by Christian subcultural norms and standards that sometimes have little or nothing to do with the will of God. And as individuals, we all have our pet rules and regulations that define the Christian experience. But the bottom line for the Christian is not, What does my church want me to do? or, What does my fellowship group want me to do? Instead, it is, What does God require of me? What is it that I am called to do to be pleasing to God?

In the new covenant, those who are in Christ have been redeemed from the curse of the law. We know that we cannot be redeemed by counting on our good works or our obedience. But we also know that we have been redeemed unto righteousness, and that the goal of the Christian life is righteousness. How do we know what righteousness looks like? We must look at the brightest and clearest revelation of righteousness, which is found in the law of God.

The psalmist said, "Oh how I love your law!" (Ps. 119:97). He delighted in the law of the Lord because he delighted in the Lord, and he wanted to learn how he could please God. If a Christian today says, "I don't care about the Old Testament law," that is tantamount to saying, "I don't care about pleasing God." Is it even possible for a person to truly to be in Christ and yet have no concern for doing what is pleasing to God?

Jesus made clear the abiding significance of the law in terms of pleasing God when He said, "If you love me, you will keep my commandments" (John 14:15). At the end of His exposition of the Ten Commandments and the deeper meaning of the law of God in the Sermon on the Mount, Jesus closed with a terrifying warning: "Not everyone who says to me, 'Lord, Lord,' will enter the kingdom of heaven, but the one who does the will of my Father who is in heaven. On that day many will say to me, 'Lord, Lord, did we not prophesy in your name, and cast out demons in your name, and do many mighty works in your name?' And then will I declare to them, 'I never knew you; depart from me, you workers of lawlessness'" (Matt. 7:21–23).

The people about whom Jesus was talking claim an intimate relationship with Christ, but Jesus replies that He does not know them, and He calls them "workers of lawlessness." That is a dreadful commentary on antinomianism of any form. For Jesus, obeying God was His life. It was His meat and His drink. Zeal for His Father's house consumed Him. So why would He delight in those who despise the things that He loves?

The New Testament calls us to grow up into maturity in Christ, to be conformed to the image of Christ, and to seek the mind of Christ. To have the mind of Christ means that we think like Christ so that we act like Christ. The New Testament calls us to the *imitatio Christi*—the imitation of Christ—and the Apostle Paul sets forth the idea that we are to imitate Christ as Christ imitated the Father. How did Jesus do that? By His perfect obedience. We as believers are to imitate Jesus' zeal for pleasing the Father. And there is no better place to learn what is pleasing to God and what He wants His people to do than by looking in His law.

The Decalogue, or Ten Commandments, is like the Magna Carta of the Old Testament law. In regard to forms of law, there are two basic types: apodictic and casuistic. Casuistic law is case law. Case law is drawn from precedents, wherein similar prior incidents and their judgments are used to inform the case at hand. In the Old Testament, laws of this type are usually written in an "if-then" style: for example, if an ox tramples his neighbor's wheat field, then the owner of the ox must pay certain damages to the neighbor. Case law spells out the implications of the apodictic law.

Apodictic law is the foundational, fundamental law that governs the people. It is communicated as personal commands or prohibition, and it carries the force of the moral absolute. The apodictic law of Old Testament Israel is found in the Ten Commandments. They were the foundational precepts that governed the land of Israel. They were Israel's constitution.

In addition to being apodictic, the form of the Ten Commandments are also *elliptical*, meaning that they contain something that is not stated in addition to that which is stated. The unstated content is assumed and can legitimately be inserted. The primary elliptical character of the law of God—which we can see by seeing how Jesus expounds the Ten Commandments in the Sermon on the Mount—is that when the law of God prohibits one thing, it at the same time silently, tacitly enjoins or requires its opposite. And conversely, when it enjoins something, it at the same time prohibits its opposite.

For example, when the first commandment says, "You shall have no other gods before me" (Ex. 20:3), it is stated negatively—"You shall not." We are not allowed to have any gods before the true God, and the opposite would be to have gods before Him. The commandment tacitly commands us to give our entire devotion singularly and consistently to God and to God alone.

This gets a little more complex and subtle when the law states something such as, "You shall not murder" (Ex. 20:13). What does this require of us? Jesus explained in the Sermon on the Mount that it does not simply mean that we are not permitted to murder. Rather, it means everything from "Do not murder" to "Do promote life." He clarified the wider implications by saying that the prohibition against murder also means that we must not be angry with others without just cause. We are not to hate others. But on the positive side, it also includes a tacit commandment to work for the well-being of all human life. It isn't just a negation of murder; it's a pro-life statement.

As we have seen, God's law in the Ten Commandments comes in the form of apodictic literary structure. It comes in the form of an absolute personal obligation—"you shall" and "you shall not." And it comes with elliptical character. These components are important to understand as we begin to look at the individual commands.

Chapter Six

No Other Gods

Having established that Old Testament law is still relevant to New Testament Christians, we can now begin to look at the Ten Commandments in detail, study their meaning, and consider how they apply to our daily lives.

In Exodus 20, we read: "And God spoke all these words, saying, 'I am the LORD your God, who brought you out of the land of Egypt, out of the house of slavery. You shall have no other gods before me'" (vv. 1–3). The opening statements of this verse include the preamble and prologue to the law, whereby God identifies Himself as the Lawgiver: "I am the LORD your God, who brought you out of the land of Egypt." Traditionally, the final portion of the verse is seen as the first commandment: "You shall have no other gods before me."

Some scholars say that this commandment affirms that the Israelites acknowledged other deities, but that they were to direct their supreme allegiance and devotion to Yahweh. The surrounding cultures operated this way—there were many gods, and each nation was seen as having its own tribal god to whom they were primarily devoted. Yahweh, these scholars say, was simply the tribal God of the Israelites.

However, classical orthodox Christianity rejects this view and teaches instead that the concept of monotheism—belief in one true God—is found right at the beginning of the Ten Commandments. Here, we see a God who is not simply Lord over a given people or particular nation, but a God who is the Creator of heaven and earth and all that is within them.

The commandment does not simply prohibit polytheism or idolatry; it prohibits even the acknowledgment of other gods, even if the Lord God is given pride of place.

"Before" does not mean "ahead of in rank." It means that we are not to have any gods before God's face or in His presence. When we consider that God's presence is universal and that He is omnipresent, we see that there is nowhere we could go where we would be allowed to worship other gods. The first commandment says that God will not allow His glory and His name to be shared with anything in the created order. God and God alone is to be Lord of the nations, and He alone is to be worshiped.

In his *Institutes of the Christian Religion*, John Calvin noted four elements of this prohibition against having any other gods in the presence of the true God. The basic principle of the first commandment is that nothing that belongs to God is to be ascribed or attributed to any other thing, and the four elements that belong to God exclusively, according to Calvin, are adoration, trust, invocation, and thanksgiving.

All of Scripture emphasizes the need to come before God in a spirit of reverence, praise, honor, and above all, worship. It is the duty of every person to worship the God who is, and worship means ascribing to Him the honor and glory due His name. To ascribe that honor and glory to any other thing is idolatry.

If we look at the Old Testament, we see that the root problem of Israelite religion was the constant flirtation with idols. Yet, the Israelites have not been the only people to seek after idols. In the first chapter of Romans, the Apostle Paul teaches that the fundamental, primordial sin—not just of Israel but of all mankind—is the sin of idolatry, in which the glory that belongs exclusively to God is exchanged for a lie, and people worship and serve the creature rather than the Creator. Creature worship lies at the heart of idolatry. We must be careful with this definition, however, for we have a tendency to think of idolatry simply in crass and primitive terms of bowing down before an idol, such as the golden calf or a totem pole. In reality, idolatry takes place when any attribute of God is stripped from His glory, and we replace the biblical God with a god that we create in our own image.

For example, the Bible reveals that God is altogether holy. He is a God of pure righteousness, justice, mercy, wrath, and love. If we begin to play fast and loose with these attributes and concoct a God who is stripped of His sovereignty, holiness, omnipotence, or immutability, we are in essence exchanging the glory and truth of God for a lie. We fail to honor God as God, and that is precisely Paul's indictment in Romans 1. The wrath of God is revealed against all those who take away from the true glory of His character and refuse to adore Him as the God who truly is.

All of us, to a greater or lesser degree, allow elements of idolatry to intrude into our faith and religion. If we don't like certain aspects of who God is and we blot out those attributes from our understanding of His character, then the God we're worshiping is not the true God. We cannot pick and choose the attributes of God that we happen to like and discard the ones we don't, for then we are constructing a false god. The true God is the God who reveals Himself in sacred Scripture.

Second, Calvin noted that not only is worship to be ascribed to God and God alone, but so also is trust. What Calvin meant by this is not that we can't trust people on a human level. Rather, he meant that the ultimate trust we cling to for our salvation must be in God. We may be tempted to trust in many things that are not God: ourselves, the church, our friends, or our labors. But our trust must rest ultimately in God, who alone is trustworthy in the ultimate sense.

The third element that Calvin said belongs to God alone is invocation. The word *invocation* refers to calling upon. On whom do we call for comfort, rescue, and fulfillment as human beings? Do we say we believe in, trust, and worship God, but then appeal to the stars, our ancestors, or to something else to redeem us? Our reliance must ultimately be on God and the help we receive from Him.

The fourth aspect of worship that belongs to God alone, according to Calvin, is thanksgiving. Returning to Romans 1, Paul says that while God reveals Himself through creation, men suppress this truth in unrighteousness and fall into idolatry. He convicts mankind of two particular evils: the refusal to honor God as God and the failure to give thanks to God. In other words, there is another sin that accompanies the primary sin of the fallen human race: in addition to refusing to adore, honor, and worship God, we also refuse to be thankful to God.

One way this lack of gratitude manifests itself is when we murmur and complain about our situation in this world. Sometimes we harbor within our hearts the idea that God is not being fair, that we deserve a better lot than we currently enjoy, and that the problem lies ultimately with God. We focus on our problems and troubles and begin to think that God has been unfair to us, rather than understanding that every good and perfect gift we enjoy in this life comes from Him. For every benefit that we receive from His hand, we should be quick to respond with thanksgiving, praise, and honor. If we are ungrateful, we violate the first commandment because we are not keeping God, who is rich in mercy and goodness, before our eyes. We are not worshiping Him with the praise of our thanksgiving and gratitude.

We weren't created simply for our work, health, happiness, marriages, or relationships. All of those are part of the riches of life as we know it, but the ultimate end for which we were created is to glorify God. That's why the very first commandment calls us to that very task. God is jealous for His name, and we have been created for His glory.

Chapter Seven

No Idols

In the last chapter, we saw that the first commandment excludes all forms of idolatry. But lest we think that a prohibition against idolatry is merely an implication of the first commandment, the second commandment speaks explicitly and directly to the issue of idolatry.

The second commandment states:

You shall not make for yourself a carved image, or any likeness of anything that is in heaven above, or that is in the earth beneath, or that is in the water under the earth. You shall not bow down to them or serve them, for I the LORD your God am a jealous God, visiting the iniquity of the fathers on the children to the third and the fourth generation of those who hate me, but showing steadfast love to thousands of those who love me and keep my commandments. (Ex. 20:4–6)

At first glance, this command may seem like a universal prohibition against forming any images whatsoever. In fact, some have taken the commandment to mean that God repudiates art. Interpreting the command in this way extends the question beyond restrictions on art in the worship of God to whether art itself is a legitimate endeavor. The commandment does say "any likeness of anything" in the heaven above, the earth beneath, or the water under the earth.

When we face this type of question of interpretation, it is important to recognize that any given text of Scripture must be understood in light of the whole counsel of God. When we look at what the rest of Scripture teaches regarding this command, we see that it cannot be a blanket prohibition of art, for then God would be contradicting Himself. When God commissioned the construction of the Old Testament tabernacle, and later the temple in Jerusalem, the Holy Spirit ordained, instituted, commanded, and enabled the people to create valuable pieces of art. Therefore, based on other passages of Scripture, we may not conclude that this commandment prohibits all art. In fact, if we consider the Most Holy Place (the innermost chamber of the temple), we see that the mercy seat on the top of the ark of the covenant, which was considered God's throne on earth, is capped off with images of angelic beings who stretch their wings out over the ark. That fact alone should give us pause when rushing to conclude that all art is prohibited by God.

However, what is clearly involved in this commandment is a prohibition against making images that are meant to be replica manifestations of God Himself. A prime example is the golden calf that the Israelites prevailed upon Aaron to make (at the very time, ironically, that God was delivering the commandments to Moses). In crass forms of idolatry such as this, people begin to worship and venerate the images themselves, not the God they are meant to represent.

To prevent this worship of earthly things, God prohibits man from making any images of Him, because He, by nature, is invisible. He is a spirit, and He is to be worshiped in spirit and in truth. And the essence of idolatry, as we saw in Romans 1, is the exchanging of the truth of God's glory for a lie by serving and worshiping creatures. These creatures include not only the creatures of nature but also the objects that we make with our own hands.

Even a cursory reading of the Old Testament prophets reveals God's extreme denunciation of the practice. Pagan nations were judged, as were the children of Israel. God's people, in disobedience, used the high places in the worship of sacred images and statues. Isaiah and Jeremiah, for example, ridiculed the practice of idolatry by saying, in effect: "You people make and forge objects with your own hands out of deaf and dumb objects of wood or of stone, and then after you have shaped them, you begin to talk to them as if they could hear, you begin to pray to them as if they could answer your prayers. This is madness; you are behaving in a manner toward the images that is appropriate only in the presence of God Himself" (see Isa. 44:9–20; Jer. 10).

Calvin said that fallen man, by nature, is a *fabricum idolarum*, meaning "idol factory." We're not prone to occasionally and accidentally getting involved in the making of idols—we are idol factories. We continually manufacture rivals to God for our devotion.

One of the great disputes during the Reformation in the sixteenth century centered on the use and function of images and statues in worship. In the sixteenth century, images, icons, and idols were an integral part of the worship of the Roman Catholic Church. The churches were filled with statues of Mary and the saints, and people came into the church and said prayers in front of the statues. The Roman Catholic Church asserted that icons were not to be worshiped, for they understood that the Bible prohibits idolatry. The word *idolatry* is a combination of two Latin words: *idolum* and *latria*. *Latria* means worship, so the church prohibited overt worship of idols. However, Rome argued that it is acceptable to engage in *idola dulia*. *Dulia* means "slavery" or "service." The Roman Catholic Church distinguished between what it saw as two different acts: *idola dulia* is appropriate, but *idola latria* is prohibited. That is, people can render service to—that is, venerate—the statues but not worship them.

The Reformers, however, protested against this understanding, arguing that it is a distinction without a difference. When people prostrate themselves and venerate statues of stone or wood, what is the difference between doing that and worshiping them? In addition, Rome claimed that the Virgin Mary should receive not only *dulia*, but *hyperdulia*. Not only is service to be rendered to Mary, but an extreme form of service is to be given to her. That was part of the protest of the Reformation.

In response to the perceived idolatry of Rome, some of the Reformers went to great lengths to remove all statues, stained-glass windows, and almost every form of art from their churches. Their motive was to place the attention in worship back on the true character of God. They reasoned that if they were to err in this matter, it was better to err in the direction of too little art rather than too much, since the propensity of the flesh is to confuse the image with what it represents. Some churches even went so far as to remove crosses from their sanctuaries, lest the people begin to worship the symbol rather than what it points to.

Calvin, on the other hand, argued that art depicting real historical events is legitimate. What the church has to guard against, according to the commandment, is any attempt to render God in any concrete form. For example, consider Michelangelo's painting of creation in the Sistine Chapel ceiling. Most of us are familiar with that magnificent fresco of a muscular deity reaching from the heavens with His outstretched index finger, touching the finger of Adam. The Reformers would have considered this work of art a violation of the second commandment, because it depicts God in human form. That is an image of the invisible God.

The heart of the matter of the second commandment is basically the same as that of the first commandment: we are to honor God as He is, not making any substitute that would direct or deflect our attention and worship away from Him. By implication, the second commandment is also a prohibition against superstition. Idolatry and super-stition often go hand in hand because people begin to impart the power of magic to elements of the created order. The Old Testament law clearly shows how important it is to God that His people not be involved in superstition.

In every age, in every generation, and in every religious denomination, there is a pervasive and perennial danger that faith will become infused with superstitious elements. This problem of mixing religion with superstition has been present since the fall of man, and no religion in the world is com-pletely free of superstition. As man has a propensity toward idolatry, he also has a certain fascination toward magic.

We should remember Luther's statement: "Let God be God." This simply means that we must keep the character of God in front of our eyes at all times, not seeking to alter it or trying to appropriate the powers of God to ourselves. We are not God. Our pastors are not God. Our church is not God. Let God be God, and let us worship Him and live in His presence according to His Word.

Chapter Eight

Don't Misuse the Name of God

The third commandment issues this prohibition: "You shall not take the name of the LORD your God in vain, for the LORD will not hold him guiltless who takes his name in vain" (Ex. 20:7). In this sober warning, God reminds His people that violators will be held accountable: He will not regard as guiltless those who use His name in vain. This fact is worth emphasizing, for the violation of the third commandment is one of the most common sins in our culture today—not only in the secular arena but in the religious sphere as well.

What does it mean to take the name of the Lord in vain? In the English language, the word *vanity* is used as a synonym for pride or narcissism, but when the Old Testament speaks of vanity, it is a synonym for *futility*. Therefore, the command means that God's name is sacred and not to be treated in a cavalier or trivial manner, but rather in a careful and guarded way.

Lest we think that the third commandment doesn't have any significance to New Testament Christians, we need only look at the Lord's Prayer to be disabused of that notion. The very first petition that Jesus instructed people to pray was that God's name be regarded as holy— "Hallowed be your name" (Matt. 6:9). We are to treat God's name as holy because it is *His* name, and we are to regard Him as holy. A cavalier attitude toward God's name reveals more about us than any of our creeds do, for it shows the deepest attitudes of our hearts toward Him.

The most obvious violation of this command, of course, is a blasphemous use of God's name, and God takes blasphemy very seriously. In Old Testament Israel, blaspheming the name of God was a capital offense. Even in our own country's history, blasphemy was once punishable by law. But we are no longer living in a time when the state regards us as guilty if we blaspheme the name of God. What was a capital offense in Israel is no offense at all in the American judicial system today. While there is still a modicum of censorship on public broadcast television, those restrictions do not apply to the name of God. We can watch television and hear the name of God blasphemed thirty times in thirty minutes. The civil magistrate in our day may hold guiltless the person who blasphemes the name of God, but God will not hold guiltless one who does.

The third commandment also extends beyond these obvious violations to ones that would be less apparent to us today (but which would have been clear to the Old Testament Jews). God's name can also be taken in vain in the use of vows and oaths. Because of the propensity of human beings to break promises and violate each other's trust, promise-making was elevated to a higher degree of seriousness in ancient Israel, where the promise was sanctified by an oath or a vow. A promise was not just a casual statement of intent but a solemn declaration.

Many of our relationships in this world are defined in terms of promises, agreements, and covenants. Our relationships with our employers are industrial contracts. The relationships we enter into in sales agreements with merchants, in which we promise to pay in a certain period of time, are covenants. Marriages are based upon promises certified by sacred vows and oaths.

When these promises were made in Israel, the people swore a vow or took a sacred oath by appealing to God as the witness between the parties. A modern-day comparison would be the question we hear in a court of law: "Do you swear to tell the truth, the whole truth, and nothing but the truth, so help you God?" In saying, "So help me God," we are appealing to God to be the final judge of our truthfulness.

Jesus took the swearing of vows and oaths very seriously and gave instruction on how to take—and how not to take—vows and oaths (Matt. 5:33–37). The book of James tells us that the word of Christians should be trustworthy and that people should be able to take us at our word (5:12).

The third commandment does not, however, preclude all vows. More than once in the New Testament, the

Apostle Paul gives testimony and swears to his truthfulness by taking an oath in the name of God. Oaths such as these are legitimate, but swearing by the earth, by the heavens, or on our mothers' graves is not, because when we swear by such things, we are slipping into a form of idolatry. If a person swears on his mother's grave to verify his words, his mother's grave has no power to enforce that promise. It is an empty promise. And when we swear by things that are less than God, we attribute to those things the very power of God Himself. We act as though the grave can do what only God can do, and therefore we commit an act of idolatry.

Oaths are to be taken in the name of God if they are to be legitimate because the swearing of lawful vows and oaths is in itself an act of worship. We are bearing witness to our faith that God can hear all things and see all things—that He is omniscient, omnipresent, and omnipotent. He has the power to judge between us, and He has the authority to be the final arbiter among people.

When we swear by God, we are acknowledging Him to be God; thus even in this commandment, we see a reinforcement of the same concern present in the first and second commandments—namely, the prohibition against all forms of idolatry. If we have a true faith and an accurate understanding of what it means to honor, glorify, and worship God, not only will we treat Him as God directly, but also in how we use His name, both privately and publicly. And this is not simply a religious thing; it has to do with all of life being lived under the recognition of the transcendent majesty and excellency of God.

A final way in which this prohibition is violated is in attributing to the name of God impulses and direction that don't come from Him at all. People say, "The Lord led me to do this," or, "The Lord spoke to me and told me to do this." This has become acceptable spiritual behavior in the Christian community to the point that it would be considered impolite for someone to respond, "How do you know that God has spoken to you?"

If by saying this people meant that they were reading the Scripture, and as they read they came under conviction from a certain text, that would be fine. But if they mean to say that while driving their cars down the street they had an intuition, and now they have a plan that supposedly came from God, that's another story. That's exactly what the false prophets of Israel did in the Old Testament, preaching their own dreams instead of the words of God. If we ever say to another person that God told us to do or say something, we had better have sound reason for doing so. Otherwise, we're violating the third commandment.

Chapter Nine

Rest

As a boy growing up in Pennsylvania, I never heard the sound of a lawn mower on Sundays. Every store in our town was closed except one—the drugstore. Even then, the only part of the drugstore that was open was the pharmacy, which operated for a short period of time on Sundays to accommodate medical emergencies. In those days, the only restaurants open on Sundays were associated with hotels, where people had to be able to eat while away from home. This was a normal way of life not so very long ago. However, today this notion seems almost humorous. Sunday is now regarded almost the same as any other day of the week.

Despite this clear cultural shift in America, an important question remains for believers: What is our duty in regard to keeping the Sabbath? This is the concern of the fourth commandment. The commandment reads:

> Remember the Sabbath day, to keep it holy. Six days you shall labor, and do all your work, but the seventh day is a Sabbath to the LORD your God. On it you shall not do any work, you, or your son, or your daughter, your male servant, or your female servant, or your livestock, or the sojourner who is within your gates. For in six days the LORD made heaven and earth, the sea, and all that is in them, and rested on the seventh day. Therefore the LORD blessed the Sabbath day and made it holy. (Ex. 20:8–11)

There are disputes not only between Christians and secular people on the topic of Sabbath observance but also within the Christian community itself. Nor is this question restricted to the modern age—it has been grappled with throughout centuries of church history.

Augustine of Hippo said that nine out of the Ten Commandments were reiterated in the New Testament law of

Christ. The fourth commandment, he thought, had been abrogated—or at least certain elements of it—since the New Testament community shifted its corporate worship from the seventh to the first day of the week to commemorate the resurrection of Christ. Though the church still met on a cyclical basis of one day in seven, Augustine argued that the association of that to the seventh day of the week had changed. Along the same lines, the Apostle Paul's statements about not being bound by new moons and Sabbaths (Col. 2:16) have led many of the great teachers of the church to believe that with the coming of Christ, the whole institution of the Sabbath was set aside.

However, for the most part, the church has embraced the belief that the essential elements of Sabbath observation are still in effect. One of the arguments supporting this view is the belief that Sabbath observance was not first instituted at Mount Sinai with the giving of the commandments to the people of Israel through Moses. Instead, it was a commandment established in creation when God hallowed the seventh day. Therefore, as a creation ordinance, it is not limited to the history of Israel—the whole creation is expected to observe this day in a twofold manner: ceasing from ordinary labor and worshiping, praising, and honoring the Creator.

The fourth commandment reads, "Remember the Sabbath day, to keep it holy" (Ex. 20:8). Note that it does not say, "From this point on, the Sabbath should be regarded as holy." Instead, it says to remember that it is already holy; the command is simply to keep it that way. In the most elementary sense, to be holy means to be different. God is saying: "Remember to keep this day different. This is the one day that I have consecrated and set apart."

The first thing that makes the Sabbath different, unusual, or extraordinary is seen in Scripture's emphasis on the Sabbath as a day of rest. This does not mean that we are to sleep all day or spend twenty-four hours in total inactivity. Instead, it denotes a rest from normal labor, and as such, the Sabbath is an imitation of God's actions in creation, wherein He labored over six successive days and rested on the seventh. One of the reasons we rest is to reflect the image of God and to remember our Creator and His labor of creation—we're honoring God, not indulging ourselves.

There are obvious practical benefits to rest as well. The Israelites experienced greater physical and emotional well-being when they took a day away from difficult labor and toil. As human beings, we need rest. In fact, we were constituted in such a way that every day we must lie down and sleep in order to survive and function.

God appoints not only this daily period of time for sleep in the cycle of life but also a weekly pattern of rest from our normal labors. God was concerned that His people not be exploited or reduced to slaves who never had any opportunity for recreation, refreshment, and rest from their toil, so He appointed one day every week where people were not supposed to work. This applied not only to businessmen, merchants, and farmers but also to servants and slaves.

Further, the command applied not only to people but to beasts of burden as well. It even extended beyond living creatures to the land itself. God instituted a sabbath for the land so that it would not become despoiled through exhaustion. Every seven years, there was to be a sabbatical year on the land so that the fields could lie fallow and recover.

The second thing that is different about the Sabbath is that it was set aside for corporate worship and giving special attention to the things of God. This does not mean that for six days people should go about their business and not give God a second thought. We are not to ignore His existence for six days and then tip our hats to Him one day a week. The life of faith is to be lived every day, and all days are conducive to the worship of God. But for ancient Israel, the Sabbath was a special time of corporate worship.

We tend to be very individualistic in America, but the Christian faith is very much corporate in its orientation. We are part of a group that comes together on the Sabbath day for a solemn assembly. We gather to celebrate not only creation but also our redemption—to celebrate the resurrection of Christ and the gift of salvation that God has given to His people—and to honor God and enjoy His presence.

The third thing that is different about the Sabbath, and one that the New Testament frequently mentions, is that the Sabbath day is in itself a kind of sacrament. It's an outward sign that points to an aspect of our redemption. In the New Testament, particularly in the book of Hebrews, the Sabbath points to the final goal of our redemption: our entrance into heaven. When we enter into heaven, we are entering into our rest.

We long for the peace of heaven—not a rest of unconsciousness or oblivion, but rest from all of the cares and troubles and pains that besiege us in this mortal flesh. Every time we come together to worship on the Sabbath day, we not only remember God's work of creation but we involve ourselves in the sacramental sign of His promise of redemption. The Sabbath is to be a taste of heaven, the place where there will be no tears, no death, and no darkness. Heaven will be full of activity, but it will be the end of restlessness and anxiety, a place where we will enter a peace that transcends all human understanding. The Sabbath is meant to point to all of these realities.

The fourth commandment says not to do any work, and the Pharisees, of course, took that to an absolute degree. In response, Jesus had to instruct them about the work that may be done on the Sabbath day. It is lawful to do good on the Sabbath day. If someone's animal falls into a pit, it shouldn't be left there to die. If a person becomes sick on the Sabbath day, we don't refuse to give him medical care until the Sabbath is over. It is not only lawful but necessary to do these works of mercy and to seek to preserve life. The church has always understood that some kinds of labor are necessary on the Sabbath day. God judged Israel for working on the Sabbath only with respect to unnecessary labor and commerce where the motive for the labor was strictly economic rather than humanitarian. That's why we believe hospitals can be open on the Sabbath day, and it's certainly legitimate for the minister to work on the Sabbath day because corporate worship is part of his responsibility.

Perennial questions abound over what is considered proper and improper behavior on the Sabbath day. Arguments are endless about whether it's OK to go on a picnic or engage in various other forms of recreation on the Sabbath. Such questions will never go away, so we must be careful not to fall into the trap of the Pharisees with their legalistic approach to the Sabbath day.

The fundamental question we must stay focused on is this: Do we honor God with the Sabbath day? Are we in tune with the original purpose of the Sabbath day? Is the Sabbath any different for us than the other six days of the week? Do we look forward to Sunday not because it's the day we can sleep in and go to the beach, but rather because we get a time of refreshment from normal commerce and can have our souls refreshed by corporate worship and can be in the special presence of our Creator and Redeemer?

Chapter Ten

Respect
Your Parents

Imagine if the United States government somehow collapsed without warning, and you were given the critical task of writing a new constitution. There's only one catch: you can only choose ten laws on which to base the foundation of a new society. What laws would you choose?

Perhaps you'd have a law protecting the sanctity of life and prohibiting murder. Or, maybe you would protect private property by prohibiting theft. But who would include in his top ten laws prohibitions against coveting or abusing the name of God? And how many people would find it important to include a law that commands giving honor to parents?

The fifth commandment says this: "Honor your father and your mother, that your days may be long in the land that the LORD your God is giving you" (Ex. 20:12). As we've already noted, the Ten Commandments were the constitution for God's people. When we look at these commandments from the vantage point of twenty-first-century culture and society, there are clearly some surprises to our modern sensibilities.

Even from a secular sociological perspective, the most fundamental of all organizational units that make up a society is the family. The family unit is not unique to Western civilization; it is part of the fabric of humanity throughout the ages. But today, this foundational unit of organized living is in jeopardy. More and more people are abandoning marriage and paternal and maternal responsibilities, and we're seeing a profound sense of alienation within the family—not only between husbands and wives but also between parents and children. Given the ramifications of the loss of family cohesion, it really shouldn't surprise us that when God established the foundation for a holy nation, He included a mandate about relationships within the family.

The fifth commandment includes a word that today might be seen as archaic: *honor*. This word is fast disappearing from our vocabulary, but previous generations rightly understood the importance of honor to a well-functioning society. God understood that to maintain the structure of society, there must be a sense of honor at its core, and this is why the concept of honor is central throughout Scripture. We are called to honor the king and those who exercise civil authority over us. We are called to honor pastors and elders who exercise spiritual leadership and authority over us. We are even called to honor one another—not only our fellow brothers and sisters in Christ, but all people (1 Peter 2:17).

At the very heart of honor is the dimension of respect—recognizing the dignity of a person and treating him accordingly. The respect established in the Decalogue began with children's responsibilities toward their parents. This is where the whole concept of showing respect to divinely constituted levels of authority begins. This honor is, first, an acknowledgement that God has delegated to parents a certain authority by which the home is to be governed. That's why in the New Testament, the mandate is given to children again: "Children, obey your parents in the Lord, for this is right" (Eph. 6:1). It is part of the structure of authority that God has built into His universe. Children are not to rule the home; children are to be in submission to their parents. And not only are they to give submission and obedience to their parents, they are to give it respectfully. In other words, they are to give honor to their parents.

It is the duty of children, before God, to honor their parents. It is the duty of parents to teach the children what honor and respect mean, and if the children grow up to behave in a disrespectful manner, it is possible that the parents haven't instructed them and demanded honor and respect in the home. Of course, there comes a time when the children are no longer living under the roof of their parents and are no longer called upon to obey them in the same way that they did while they were young. But the mandate to honor our father and mother never ends. If you look at the customs in Israel, you'll see how families showed respect to the matriarch or patriarch. When the father walked into a room, it was the custom of all the children, even the adult children, to rise to show their respect and honor.

What is your gut reaction when you hear the word *honor*? People may laugh at us for even considering this a virtue anymore, but one need not be religious to understand the value of human dignity and the value of showing respect to each other, to those who are in authority over us, and particularly within the bounds of the family. As parents, do we not want the respect of our children? Don't we feel embarrassed for the ways in which we have failed to honor our own parents?

We may say, "But my father was not an honorable man," or "My mother was not an honorable woman," but God doesn't say, "Honor your father or mother only when they're honorable." They hold a position, an office, and even if they're unworthy of that office, the office itself is still to be honored. As Christians, we should be scrupulous in demonstrating honor, dignity, and respect to our parents, and by doing so, we obey God by obeying the fifth commandment.

Chapter Eleven

Protect
Human Life

The sixth commandment simply states, "You shall not murder" (Ex. 20:13). This prohibition seems simple to understand, but its ramifications have resulted in numerous controversies in church history—particularly as it relates to issues such as capital punishment, warfare, and abortion. Also significant is the fact that Jesus Himself gave an important exposition on this command in the Sermon on the Mount:

You have heard that it was said to those of old, "You shall not murder; and whoever murders will be liable to judgment." But I say to you that everyone who is angry with his brother will be liable to judgment; whoever insults his brother will be liable to the council; and whoever says, "You fool!" will be liable to the hell of fire. So if you are offering your gift at the altar and there remember that your brother has something against you, leave your gift there before the altar and go. First be reconciled to your brother, and then come and offer your gift. (Matt. 5:21–24)

In the Sermon on the Mount, Jesus frequently uses the phrase, "You have heard that it was said. . . ." This statement is an example of what we call an *idiom*, a phrase with a precise meaning that isn't always apparent to those outside the culture where the phrase is used. One of the most difficult things to translate from language to language is the idiom, and if you've ever had to learn a foreign language, you know how difficult idioms can be.

Another idiom in the Bible is the phrase "It is written." It does not refer simply to a statement that appears in print somewhere. Rather, to the Jew, the phrase meant that something had been written in a specific place—namely, in the Scriptures. For an Old Testament Jew to say, "It is written," was the equivalent of a Christian's saying, "The Bible says."

Why is this significant? Because when Jesus says, "You have heard that it was said . . . ," He is referencing the *halakha*, the oral tradition of the rabbis. There was sacred Scripture, and there was also the rabbinic interpretation of the Scripture, which was passed on from generation to generation through oral recitation. Among the Pharisees in particular, this oral tradition became elevated to a level equaling the authority of Scripture. Jesus rebuked them when they substituted the traditions of men for the law of God, and the tradition that they often substituted for the law of God was this oral tradition.

When Jesus challenges traditions in the New Testament, He never challenges what is written in the text of Scripture. He does, however, challenge the way that the biblical text had been handled and distorted in the oral tradition. So, when He speaks about the law in the Sermon on the Mount, He says, "You have heard that it was said to those of old, 'You shall not murder'" (Matt. 5:21). In this instance, Jesus is criticizing the rabbinic, pharisaical understanding of the law of God. He is not criticizing the law; He is criticizing the misinterpretation of the law. That's why He says on this same occasion, "Do not think that I have come to abolish the Law or the Prophets; I have not come to abolish them but to fulfill them" (v. 17).

The Pharisees had focused almost exclusively on the letter of the law, and as a result, they prided themselves in being law keepers if they had never committed murder. And what Jesus pointed out was that there is a deeper obligation imposed by the sixth commandment than simply the prohibition against physical murder. If a person is angry at his brother without just cause, that person has violated the sixth commandment.

We can almost hear the Pharisees object: just because someone is angry with his brother doesn't mean he has killed him. That is true, but even insulting a brother, calling him a fool, slandering him, or doing anything that injures him is prohibited in the wider application of the command, "You shall not murder." The negative aspect of the command includes all acts of sinful anger or hatred and unjust violence.

We noted earlier that the law is elliptical; that is, it contains tacit or implicit assumptions that are not explicitly spelled out. Therefore, not only what the law prohibits is in view, but also its opposite, which is commanded. The deepest sense of the sixth commandment means that we should do everything in our power to protect, preserve, maintain, and honor the lives of our neighbors.

The most controversial debates in Western history regarding the sixth commandment relate to capital punishment, war, and abortion. I remember when the Supreme Court lifted the ban on capital punishment in American society, leaving the states with the authority to legislate in this area. Pennsylvania, for example, reinstituted capital punishment for first-degree murder. When the legislature did this, the bill was vetoed by the governor of Pennsylvania, a professing Jew. He vetoed capital punishment on the basis that it violates the sixth commandment, claiming that the law of God is higher than the law of the state. He argued that if God says, "You shall not murder," then we must not kill by executing murderers.

The irony of this was that the penalty in the Old Testament for violating the sixth commandment was execution. Also, this principle of capital punishment for murder was not introduced at Sinai with the Ten Commandments but was established much earlier in biblical history when the creation covenant was renewed and reinstituted with Noah after the flood. God instructed Noah, "Whoever sheds the blood of man, by man shall his blood be shed, for God made man in his own image" (Gen. 9:6). This is not a descriptive statement but rather a command from God.

Capital punishment is required because man is created in the image of God, and God regards a malicious assault upon any human being as an assault upon the life of God Himself. If anyone dares to go with malice aforethought to slay another human being, then that person's life is forfeited. And the reason for that, biblically, is the sanctity of life. Human life is to be treated as so sacred that if anyone willfully and maliciously slaughters another human being, then that person is to be executed. Yet, ironically, in our own culture, opposition to capital punishment invariably rests on the argument of the sanctity of human life.

Before a person in Israel could be executed for murder, there were safeguards in place to protect against the politicization of the criminal justice system and ensure that innocent people were not executed in error or unjustly. Before a person could be executed for a capital offense, his guilt had to be confirmed by the testimony of two eyewitnesses, and those eyewitnesses were under the threat of execution themselves if they were convicted of committing perjury. Similarly, we must ensure that strong safeguards are in place in our own nation in order to guard against unjust executions.

The sixth commandment also relates to the classic debate over warfare. The New Testament makes it clear that God has given the power of the sword to earthly government. The individual is forbidden from executing vengeance for himself; only the civil magistrate is given the right and responsibility to use the sword to prosecute evildoers, and it is to be used only in the defense of the innocent and for just and righteous causes.

This is the historical basis for the Christian view of the just war theory. Men such as Thomas Aquinas and Augustine, considering war in light of the commandment, agreed that all wars are evil, but not everyone's involvement in war is evil. If an aggressive nation crosses borders and begins to kill the inhabitants of a land, it is not only the right but the duty of that nation's civil magistrate to use whatever force it has at its disposal—and the power of the sword, if necessary—to prevent the slaughter and defend the lives of its people.

This does not, however, mean that governments are

always just. Before anyone ever picks up a sword, a gun, or a bomb and uses it on another human being, he had better make sure that what his government is doing is just. Any earthly government can use the sword unjustly. We have to be careful against maintaining the attitude that what our own country's government does is always right.

A final major controversy related to the sixth commandment is the issue of abortion. It used to be that the big debate on abortion concerned whether the unborn fetus is a living being, and the debate focused on when life begins. Does it begin at conception? At three months? Does it begin when we can hear a heartbeat or detect brain waves? There have been countless debates over these questions. But the debate has now turned, in that many people are willing to grant that at a certain stage in the embryonic development, the fetus is alive. However, despite that fact, they hold that abortions are still permissible on the basis of the woman's right to choose what happens to her body.

The Christian protest against abortion is motivated by the positive implications of the command—not only does the law say, "You shall not kill," but the meaning of the law as Jesus set it forth means, "You shall do everything in your power to promote life." One thing we know for certain is that abortion does not do that. It does not promote the sanctity of human life. The embryo in the womb is an actual human life, so it is worthy of the full protection that we would give to any other innocent human life.

Because human beings are made in God's image, regard for the sanctity of human life must be chief in our minds. Before we pick up a gun to shoot someone, use an electric chair to execute someone, or pick up a scalpel to destroy an emerging human being, we had better know that we are right to do so.

Chapter Twelve

Love
Your Spouse

We live in an age that has very little respect for the sanctity of marriage. Of course, adultery was a problem long before the sexual revolution that took place in the United States in the 1960s, but now it is so commonplace that very few sanctions against it remain.

Even more surprising, though, is the lack of biblical sexual ethics in the church. Reports issued by the headquarters of various denominations claim that premarital sexual intercourse is permitted in the Christian life. Even extramarital sexual intercourse, it is argued, is part of our mature self-expression. This is troubling given the injunction in the seventh commandment: "You shall not commit adultery" (Ex. 20:14). If there is any area in which we see the modern culture on a collision course with the teaching of Scripture, it is in the area of sexual behavior.

Church history has witnessed many distortions in the matter of sexual activity. For example, the church was affected by the intrusion and influence of Greek dualism, particularly the early invasion of Manichaeism. According to dualism, anything physical is evil. Therefore, the only possible justification for a sexual relationship—even within marriage—is the continuation of the species. In other words, even within marriage, sexual union is at best a necessary evil.

While such a view is a dreadful distortion of biblical sexual ethics, it's certainly not the only distortion. Because of the various historical taboos associated with sex, many people labor under a sense of guilt for having a healthy sexual relationship within their marriages. One of the ironies of this problem is that with respect to sexual relationships, the New Testament makes clear that the sexual relationship between a husband and wife is not only permitted but commanded. It is part of what God has created, and He has declared that it is good.

God certainly did not have to design the human body in such a way that sex would be pleasurable, but He did. There is only a narrow window of time each month that a child can be conceived by a couple, yet there is a dimension of the physiology of sex that makes the desire for mating far more frequent than what is actually necessary to preserve the species. It's as if God, in nature itself as well as in His Word, is prescribing an intimate relationship in marriage that is not only spiritual, emotional, and mental, but also intensely physical.

We also see in the creation account that mankind was created in the image of God, male and female. The Bible goes into some depth to talk about the beauty and significance of this sexual relationship in creation. After God created everything in the physical world, He looked at His creation and pronounced a benediction upon it, saying it was good. The word *benediction* literally means "good saying." But what was the first malediction in Scripture? The first time God says something is bad is when He looks at Adam and says, "It is not good that the man should be alone" (Gen. 2:18). We then read the marvelous narrative of the creation of woman, a suitable companion for man, and the original ordination and institution of marriage, where we are told that there is to be a mystical union of two distinct individuals who come together to become one flesh. And we are also told in the creation account that in this original situation, the man and his wife were naked and unashamed.

Throughout Scripture, the metaphor of nakedness is used as a strong sign for shame and humiliation. Even the teaching on redemption uses this metaphorical language, insofar as we receive a covering for our nakedness by the grace of God—the righteousness of Christ. The first sin in the garden of Eden led to an awareness of this nakedness, followed by shame, a flight into hiding, and a search for a covering. Then, in the first act of divine mercy, God discovered His shameful creatures, embarrassed in their sin and aware of their nakedness, and He clothed them. Even the world of nature makes clear that there's something strange about human beings. How many other creatures on this planet go out of their way to make artificial garments to cover their natural bodies? None but humans. We are a clothed species, and yet there's something within the soul of each of us that longs for a place where we can once again be naked and unashamed.

The Bible, when it speaks of the sexual relationship, uses a phrase that is much more than simply a euphemism. It is the phrase *to know*. Adam *knew* his wife and she conceived. Abraham *knew* Sarah and she conceived. This does not mean they were introduced on the street one day and suddenly the women became pregnant. The phrase *to know* means to know another person at a profound level of intimacy.

All of us long for friends we can trust. We may have thousands of acquaintances that we've met in our lifetimes, but how many of those thousands of people would we call friends? And how many of these are loyal friends that we know will stand with us through anything? We are fortunate if we have loyal friends, but even then, for those who are married, the person with whom we are to be most intimate is our spouse. The safe refuge for human nakedness that God has ordained is marriage. Why is this so? Because nakedness involves more than the lack of physical clothing. It means being exposed to the scrutiny of another human being in our weakest, worst, and darkest moments. This is one of the reasons why divorce can be so dreadfully painful, because people going through a divorce experience the sensation that the person who knows them better than anyone else in the world has rejected them.

God provided a place where we can be naked. Even in our sinful condition, we can have a taste of heaven in terms of a safe refuge, and that refuge is marriage. There, we can be intimate. There, we can have a physical relationship as well as an emotional relationship. But God also mandated that marriage is the only place we are to experience this kind of relationship. Is God a killjoy? Does He not want us to have pleasure? No. God knows that sex is not a toy, and that it is far more than physical pleasure. It is to involve a deep, absolute, covenantal commitment.

We are desperate for intimacy, and we live in a day that is the most erotic time in American history, and perhaps in all of Western history as well, where we are bombarded with sexual stimulation such as we have never seen before. There is a constant undermining of the biblical sexual ethic. Tragically, chastity is almost as rare inside the church as it is outside of the church because the culture has collapsed with respect to the virtue of chastity.

Perhaps one reason why some churches want to change God's laws in the area of sexual behavior is because so many people are breaking those laws. But in doing this, we insult the wisdom of God. While we must be gracious, understanding, and merciful toward those who struggle with obedience to the law of God, it doesn't change the character of God, and it doesn't change the commitment that we are to have in marriage, in love, and in our sexual relationships.

In our marriages, there should be an attempt to celebrate redemption in this experience of nakedness, where we can be loved by someone who knows who we truly are. Someone who knows us on our good days and our bad days with the same level of loyalty and commitment. All of this is included behind the fence that God puts around marriage when He says, "You shall not commit adultery" (Ex. 20:14).

Chapter Thirteen

Don't Steal

Most of us have been the victim of theft. It can feel like an incredible violation to work hard to acquire something, only to have someone help himself to it illegitimately. It is the nadir of selfishness to appropriate to ourselves what lawfully belongs to someone else—to be so inconsiderate of another person's property and labor that we take for ourselves something we did not work to acquire, and we remove it from the hands of someone who did labor to enjoy it. Yet theft is one of the most common vices that we encounter in our society.

It was not by accident that when God gave the law, He

included the command, "You shall not steal" (Ex. 20:15). This law is explicitly mentioned again in the New Testament when the Apostle Paul addresses those who have come out of paganism in the gentile world and are now Christian believers within the church. He says, "Let the thief no longer steal" (Eph. 4:28). Simply stated, stealing is completely inconsistent with the Christian life.

The eighth commandment is given in succinct terms, but like the rest of the commandments, it carries far deeper implications, since stealing comes in many different forms. The most obvious is when someone breaks into our home, or when someone snatches our purse or wallet when we're walking down the road. These are obvious types of stealing, but there are other far more sophisticated ways to steal.

For example, theft can occur in the workplace—and not in the way that most of us would suspect. People can, of course, steal physical items from their place of employment, but theft can also occur through poor use of time. When we enter into a job agreement, we commit to work for a certain number of hours per day or per week, and we are given compensation in return. Therefore, the failure to perform the amount of labor we have been hired to perform is a kind of theft.

Another way that we violate the commandment against stealing is by not paying our bills when we promise to. In this country, there is no shortage of ways to try to legally get around these kinds of issues. Many people get themselves into financial trouble and, rather than working with their creditors to come to some sort of payment agreement, they declare bankruptcy. We as Christians are not to defraud people out of their just payments.

In what other ways do we steal? The most obvious one in Scripture is closely related to the previous example. In the book of Malachi, the prophet (speaking for God) asks this question to the nation of Israel: "Will man rob God?" (Mal. 3:8). It would seem that such a question is purely rhetorical, as the answer would be, "Of course not." Human beings may be inclined to rob one another, but who would have the audacity to steal from God Himself? Judgment came upon the house of Israel when God declared through the prophet Malachi that the people were robbing God. When they asked, "How have we robbed you?" the reply was, "In your tithes and contributions" (v. 8).

Statistics reveal that in the evangelical church (not the broader Christian community), only 12 percent of members tithe. God commands that 10 percent of our income be given to the work of His kingdom, which means that 88 percent of us who profess to be Christians systematically, regularly, and consistently rob God. We have been derelict in our duty to support the work of God.

The wonderful thing about the principle of tithing in the Old Testament is that God, unlike the American government, had a flat tax. God assessed every person in the community the same percentage rather than the same amount, so the widow who gave 10 percent was more obedient in giving her mite than the millionaire who gave 5 percent. Of course, the millionaire gave far more money and got far more adulation and respect in the life of the church than the widow, but the widow was obedient and the millionaire wasn't. We all have the same obligation, and it's a percentage obligation. The wealthier person has to give more money but the same percentage. This is wonderful—we all have the same responsibility. There is no graduated income tax in the kingdom of God and no politicization of the economy in the kingdom of God. Everyone has the same responsibility before God.

These are just a few of the many ways we regularly violate the commandment, "You shall not steal." From time to time, we need to assess our own behavior and ask ourselves, Are we thieves? Have we been stealing from our employer?

Have we been stealing from the merchants from whom we purchase goods or services? Have we been stealing from God? Do we steal not only money but labor? There are many ways that we can take for ourselves what does not properly belong to us.

Chapter Fourteen

Tell the Truth

In a sin-cursed world, we all know the experience of being wounded and violated in our relationships with others. Many times, this damage and destruction are a result of the violation of the ninth commandment: "You shall not bear false witness against your neighbor" (Ex. 20:16).

On the surface, the immediate concern relates to perjury in the courtroom. Just as we have a criminal justice system in our society, the structure of the courts in Israel was a serious matter. When justice is at stake and judgment is to be made, getting to the truth of a matter is critical. Before a person's guilt or innocence can be determined, the facts must be assembled and evaluated. Witnesses offer testimony, and this testimony is evaluated to determine whether it is credible.

When the stakes are high, people may be inclined not to tell the truth, the whole truth, and nothing but the truth. And when false testimony is given in a court of law, it can skew the verdict in two different directions: it can lead to a guilty person's exoneration or to an innocent person's conviction. In either case, justice is not served—particularly when false testimony is given that incriminates an innocent person. That's why God set up safeguards to protect the innocent. If an Israelite perjured himself in a capital case by falsely accusing an innocent person, then that witness was himself liable to execution. God took truth telling in court seriously.

This is a problem for us as fallen humans because Scripture makes this universal indictment: all men are liars. That doesn't mean that all people always lie, but there is not one of us who has never lied. We have all distorted the truth at some point in our lives.

The courtroom is not the only place where bearing false witness can be injurious and destructive to human relationships. In the last chapter, we considered the command,

"You shall not steal." If we compare the eighth and ninth commandments, we can see a connection between the two, and God is very much concerned throughout the Old Testament with this connection between lying and stealing.

According to Old Testament law, God required that merchants and governments use just standards and weights. Why would this matter? Suppose a merchant told his customer that he was selling him a quart of milk, but the bottle actually contained less than a quart of milk? Two sins are occurring simultaneously in this scenario. First, false witness is being given, and by that false testimony, theft is taking place—the merchant is taking more money from the customer than he says he would because he is giving less milk for the price than he said he would. The lie aids and abets the theft. And so, the God of Israel insisted that merchants tell the truth about the ingredients and products that they were selling, and He held the government accountable for ensuring a system of just weights and measures.

Another connection between lying and stealing in Israel related to the debasing of currency. For example, if the currency being used was made of gold, an unscrupulous ruler could mix cheap metals with the gold and pass off the coin as being full gold. Again, we see the use of lies in the service of theft.

The fundamental underlying principle behind the ninth commandment transcends economic exchanges and courtroom dramas because it is foundational to the entire Judeo-Christian ethic: the sanctity of truth. Not only are we not allowed to lie in a trial or lie to customers about the true contents of what we're selling them, but we must tell the truth in all things.

Advertising is an area where the truth is often elusive. We've all been exposed to the glut of advertising on television, in magazines, and in all the different media that makes all kinds of promises to us. Hopefully we've learned to discount the hype. But as Christians, we must be careful that we do not participate in the intentional falsification of the claims we make. Even if we bear false witness about good things with good intentions, we are still violating the sanctity of truth.

The ninth commandment not only prohibits perjury, lying, and deception, it especially prohibits slander and destructive gossip. Anytime that we accuse people of doing something that they did not do—whether in a courtroom or in a discussion with a friend over coffee—we are breaking the ninth commandment. Slander is a highly destructive and injurious enterprise whereby we rob people of their good name by falsely accusing them. God prohibits gossip and slander because they wound our fellow human beings. We have enough real guilt to deal with and enough real faults to answer for without having other people charge us with things that we haven't done.

The ninth commandment is not an exercise in abstraction, nor is it simply limited to courtroom testimony. It defines the importance of truth in human relationships. How have you felt when someone has lied about what you said or did? How did these false accusations affect your life? They may have cost you your job. Or, they may have cost you your standing in the community. Perhaps they had financial repercussions.

Jonathan Edwards said that when false accusations are made about us, we have a responsibility to handle the situation in the same way that Jesus did. No one in human history was ever lied about or slandered more viciously than Jesus was, but like a lamb led to the slaughter, He did not open His mouth. Not only must we refrain from bearing false witness against others, but we also need to learn how to respond when we are the victims—by following the example of Christ.

Chapter Fifteen

Be Satisfied

As we've noted throughout our study of the Decalogue, it's often puzzling to see what God chose to include in His top ten laws for the nation of Israel. The tenth commandment is no exception in this regard: "You shall not covet your neighbor's house; you shall not covet your neighbor's wife, or his male servant, or his female servant, or his ox, or his donkey, or anything that is your neighbor's" (Ex. 20:17).

The tenth commandment is not quite as terse as the previous commandments—you shall not murder, you shall not commit adultery, you shall not steal, you shall not bear false witness against your neighbor. Those commands are brief and to the point, but the tenth commandment includes some additional information. It doesn't simply state, "You shall not covet," but goes on to expand the prohibition by giving specific examples—the list is obviously representative rather than exhaustive—until finally the summary statement is made: "or anything that is your neighbor's."

What exactly is covetousness, and how do we know if we are guilty of violating this prohibition? A simple definition of coveting is wanting for yourself what properly belongs to someone else. Why would this inner feeling of vice be included in the Ten Commandments? Before we answer this question, ask yourself how many sermons you have heard on covetousness. I've spent a lot of time in churches, and I don't know how many sermons I've heard in my lifetime, but I cannot think of a single sermon I've ever heard on the sin of coveting. Yet God considers it so significant that He included it in the Ten Commandments.

The issue of covetousness is not limited in Scripture to the Ten Commandments alone. A simple perusal of the words *covet, covetousness,* and *coveting* in a Bible concordance quickly reveals the astounding frequency with which the Word of God speaks about this problem. Unfortunately, there seems to be an inverse proportional relationship between how often God speaks about coveting and how often pastors address this topic. This quite possibly means that we have failed to grasp the weighty significance of this human problem.

One way that we see the problem of covetousness is in vandalism. The motive behind vandalism is this: If I can't afford or own what you have, then you're not going to enjoy it either. In other words, a vandal seeks to make absolutely certain that no one around him can enjoy anything that he cannot personally enjoy. As in the case of stealing, this reflects a profound self-centeredness and selfishness.

It is no wonder that when asked what is the greatest commandment in the law, Jesus responded by saying, "You shall love the Lord your God with all your heart and with all your soul and with all your mind. This is the great and first commandment. And a second is like it: You shall love your neighbor as yourself" (Matt. 22:37–39). If we loved our neighbors as much as we loved ourselves, we would never steal from them or kill them. We would never bear false witness against them, nor would we covet what they possess. In our love for our neighbor, we would, as the

Apostle tells us, "rejoice with those who rejoice [and] weep with those who weep" (Rom. 12:15).

The ethic of Christ tells us that we are to prefer one another above ourselves, which is the exact opposite of covetousness. The great commandment neatly and succinctly summarizes the Ten Commandments, and the Golden Rule incorporates all of these commandments into one distilled essence: "So whatever you wish that others would do to you, do also to them, for this is the Law and the Prophets" (Matt. 7:12). If we obeyed these words of Christ, then we would never destroy someone else's property, because we don't like it when someone destroys ours.

Lurking under the surface of covetousness is a deadly sin: jealousy. Jealousy is insidious and destructive. When we are jealous of other people's accomplishments, property, possessions, or achievements, not only are we not being neighborly, we are hating our neighbors. And ultimately, jealousy is an affront to and an assault against God. If we understand that every good and perfect gift comes from above, and that it is only by divine providence that we have what we have and others have what they have, then our covetousness and jealousy reveal that we believe God was wrong to have given things to others and not to us.

In other words, we complain and murmur and blaspheme against God Himself.

That's why the Apostle Paul says, "I have learned in whatever situation I am to be content. I know how to be brought low, and I know how to abound" (Phil. 4:11–12). It's an echo of the sentiments of Job, upon whom God had bestowed untold material blessings before it was all taken away from him. Job said, "The LORD gave, and the LORD has taken away; blessed be the name of the LORD" (Job 1:21). Job understood that every good and perfect gift comes from God. And because of that, there's no reason to be jealous.

We even covet other people's honor. This is especially irrational, because it's not as though God has put a limited supply of honor in His universe. It's not a limited commodity like diamonds or gold. If we are honorable, we will receive honor, so why should we be jealous when someone else receives honor? We are to give honor where honor is due, and there's plenty of honor to go around.

Jealousy reflects a heart that does not trust in God and is not satisfied with the hand of God's providence. Jealousy fails to regard the gifts that God has given to us, and it reflects a failure to be properly grateful. If we are truly grateful to God for what He has given us, then there's no room for covetousness. And the moment we become covetous, we reveal our ingratitude toward God.

There's another reason why this sin was prohibited in Israel: covetousness is the motivating force behind so many of the other behaviors that are prohibited in the Ten Commandments. When we covet, we are only one step away from stealing. When we covet another's spouse, we are only one step away from adultery. When we covet someone else's life, we are taking a step toward murder. When we covet another's status, we are one step away from slander, gossip, and lying. God, who understands the human heart fully, had a reason for warning against covetousness: He knows that it is the pit out of which poison and venom flow into all areas of human relationships.

Despite the fact that there are far too few sermons and warnings about covetousness, we need to be aware of it the instant it shows up in our hearts. The roots of bitterness, jealousy, anger, theft, adultery, and murder are found in the heart that covets what someone else has. And so, God emphatically closes the Ten Commandments by saying, "You shall not covet . . . anything that is your neighbor's."

As the Decalogue comes to an end, we read these words:

"Now when all the people saw the thunder and the flashes of lighting and the sound of the trumpet and the mountain smoking, the people were afraid and trembled, and they stood far off and said to Moses, 'You speak to us, and we will listen; but do not let God speak to us, lest we die'" (Ex. 20:18–19). That was the first reaction to the giving of the law of God—"Do not let God speak to us"—and sadly, this is still the reaction of many of God's people, evidenced by how we remove ourselves as far as we possibly can from the teaching of the law.

In our study of God's law, we first examined the principles that govern our understanding of divine law, and then we looked individually at the Ten Commandments. We saw that the saint in the Old Testament—as well as in the New Testament—is defined as a person who loves the law of God because it is *His* law and because it reveals to us His character and His goodness. The law also reveals to us our sinfulness, and perhaps that's why we tend to minimize it or avoid it altogether.

But even the revelation of our sinfulness that we see in the mirror of the law is mercy and grace, because it has the effect of pointing us to Christ. The most astonishing thing about Jesus is not simply that He died for our violations of the law and came under the curse of the law on our behalf. The thing about Jesus that is unfathomable is that He kept the law, and He kept it perfectly. He never coveted. He never lusted. He never lied. He never cheated. He never stole. He was never angry without cause. Jesus was perfect, and He gives the benefit of His merit to all who put their trust in Him alone.

About the Author

Dr. R.C. Sproul was founder of Ligonier Ministries, founding pastor of Saint Andrew's Chapel in Sanford, Fla., first president of Reformation Bible College, and executive editor of *Tabletalk* magazine. His radio program, *Renewing Your Mind*, is still broadcast daily on hundreds of radio stations around the world and can also be heard online. He was author of more than one hundred books, including *The Holiness of God, Chosen by God,* and *Everyone's a Theologian*. He was recognized throughout the world for his articulate defense of the inerrancy of Scripture and the need for God's people to stand with conviction upon His Word.

Free eBooks *by*
R.C. Sproul

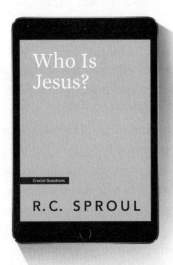

Does prayer really change things? Can I be sure I'm saved? Dr. R.C. Sproul

answers these important questions, along with more than twenty-five

others, in his Crucial Questions series. Designed for the Christian or

thoughtful inquirer, these booklets can be used for personal study, small

groups, and conversations with family and friends. Browse the collection

and download your free digital ebooks today.

Get 3 free months
of *Tabletalk*

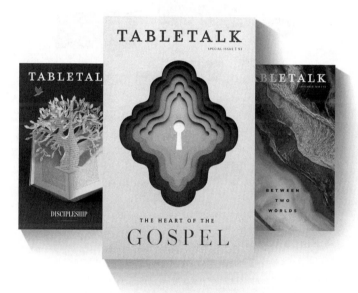

In 1977, R.C. Sproul started *Tabletalk* magazine.
Today it has become the most widely read subscriber-based monthly
devotional magazine in the world. **Try it free for 3 months.**

𝕋 TryTabletalk.com/CQ | 800.435.4343

ASK LIGONIER

Do we have free will?

Why did God kill Uzzah?

Is it true that God controls everything?

A Place to Find Answers

Maybe you're leading a Bible study tomorrow. Maybe you're just beginning to dig deeper. It's good to know that you can always ask Ligonier. For more than forty-five years, Christians have been looking to Ligonier Ministries, the teaching fellowship of R.C. Sproul, for clear and helpful answers to biblical and theological questions. Now you can ask those questions as they arise, confident that our team will work quickly to provide clear, concise, and trustworthy answers. When you have questions, just ask Ligonier.

FOR MORE INFORMATION, VISIT LIGONIER.ORG/ASK